Don't forget to visit **www.blitzbooks.com** to download lots of FREE fantastic worksheets, manuscript, flashcards and more!

CW00496424

How To ~~Pass~~ Sight Singing

Training for your eyes and ears

by Samantha Coates

Writing this book would not have been possible without the incredible input and support from Allison Harrigan and Lyn Williams. My heartfelt thanks to both of these inspirational women.

Published by
Chester Music,
part of The Music Sales Group,
14-15 Berners Street, London W1T 3LJ, UK.

Exclusive Distributors:
Music Sales Limited
Distribution Centre, Newmarket Road,
Bury St Edmunds, Suffolk IP33 3YB, UK.

Music Sales Pty Limited
4th floor, Lisgar House, 30-32 Carrington Street,
Sydney, NSW 2000, Australia.

Order No. CH85195
ISBN 978-1-78558-358-2

Your Guarantee of Quality:

As publishers, we strive to produce every book
to the highest commercial standards.

Particular care has been given to specifying acid-free,
neutral-sized paper made from pulps which have not
been elemental chlorine bleached.

This pulp is from farmed sustainable forests and was
produced with special regard for the environment.

Throughout, the printing and binding have been
planned to ensure a sturdy, attractive publication
which should give years of enjoyment.

If your copy fails to meet our high standards,
please inform us and we will gladly replace it.

www.musicsales.com

Chester Music
part of The Music Sales Group
London / New York / Paris / Sydney / Copenhagen / Berlin / Madrid / Hong Kong / Tokyo

Contents

←——————————→

Welcome to Music!

There are so many things to learn about music and the way it is written. In this book you'll be learning the 'basics' of music notation as well as how to sing what you see – which is called 'sight singing'.

Below is an example of some quite complicated music for voice and piano. As a singer, you'll pretty much always see the piano part on your music! It may all look like gobbledygook at the moment, but soon a lot of things will start to make sense.

The Apple Tree

Ask your teacher to help you find these items in the music above: stave, treble clef, bass clef, notes, rests, barlines, time signature, key signature. You don't need to know what they all mean just now, but it's good to have seen them and to have at least heard of these terms before we begin!

Crotchets and Quavers

Music notes are written in different ways. Here are three types.

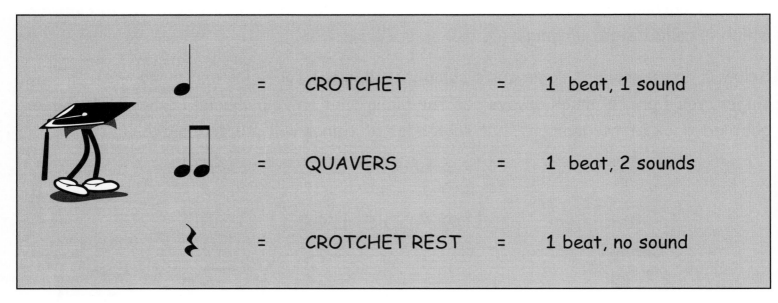

Try clapping these rhythms:

1. ♩ 𝄽 ♩ ♩

2. ♩ ♩ ♫ ♩

3. ♩ 𝄽 ♫ ♫ ♫

4. ♫ ♫ 𝄽 ♩

Notes may also have the stem going down, like this:  or this  !

Clap these!

1.

2.

3.

4.

Which Rhythm?

Here are six short rhythms, with crotchet rests, crotchets and quavers only.
Clap each one so you know what they sound like.

Your teacher will now clap or play them in a random order. See if you can number them from 1 to 6 in the boxes!

a.

d.

b.

e.

c. [image: rhythm notation — crotchet, two quavers, crotchet, crotchet]

f. [image: rhythm notation — crotchet, crotchet rest, two quavers, crotchet]

Make up your own eight-beat rhythm here. Then teach a friend how to clap it!

Sounds and Shapes

Notes that go up on the stave are getting higher:

These notes are moving up step by step. Try singing some!

Notes that go down on the stave are getting lower:

These notes are moving down step by step. Try singing some!

And notes that stay in the same spot will sound the same!

Finally, when notes leap around on the stave, the tune will have a really jumpy sound:

Things to do:

★ See if you can sing a few notes in a row that sound identical.

★ Sing some notes that start low and get gradually higher.

★ Try singing notes that sound like they are leaping around, from high to low and back again!

Listen to and sing back these melodies, then match them up with the correct description.

stepping up

stepping down

leaping up

leaping down

staying the same

going up then down

stepping down then leaping up

leaping down then stepping up

Let's Draw Treble Clefs

We're mostly using treble clef in this book, because we are singing and reading notes above middle C.

To draw a treble clef, start on the second line ⸻ , then wind around like

this ⸻ . You then need to go up past the fifth line and make a loop above the

staff. ⸻ As you come down you must intersect on the fourth line ⸻ .

★ Trace these treble clefs. Remember to start on the second line...

★ Now try drawing some treble clefs of your own. Start on the second line and make sure each one crosses over in the right spot!

DID YOU KNOW... Bass-clef notes (e.g. notes below middle C) are mostly sung by men and boys with deep voices. Try out some low notes with your teacher!

Lines and Spaces

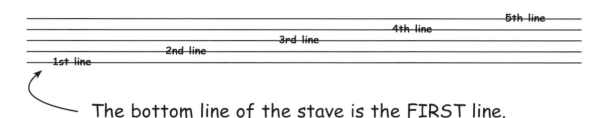

Music is written on sets of five lines called a 'staff' or 'stave'. We'll refer to it both ways throughout this book.

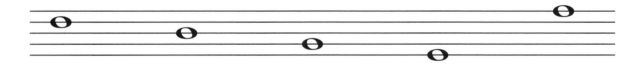

The bottom line of the stave is the FIRST line.

Here are some notes on lines. Notice how the line goes through the middle of each note!

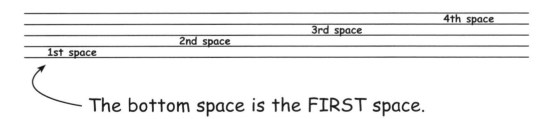

★ Find and circle the note on the third line.

In between the five lines there are four SPACES.

The bottom space is the FIRST space.

Here are some notes in spaces (between the lines).

★ Find and circle the note in the second space.

Match-Up

Match each 'sentence' to the correct oval shape... and remember that the BOTTOM line is the first line and the BOTTOM space is the first space!

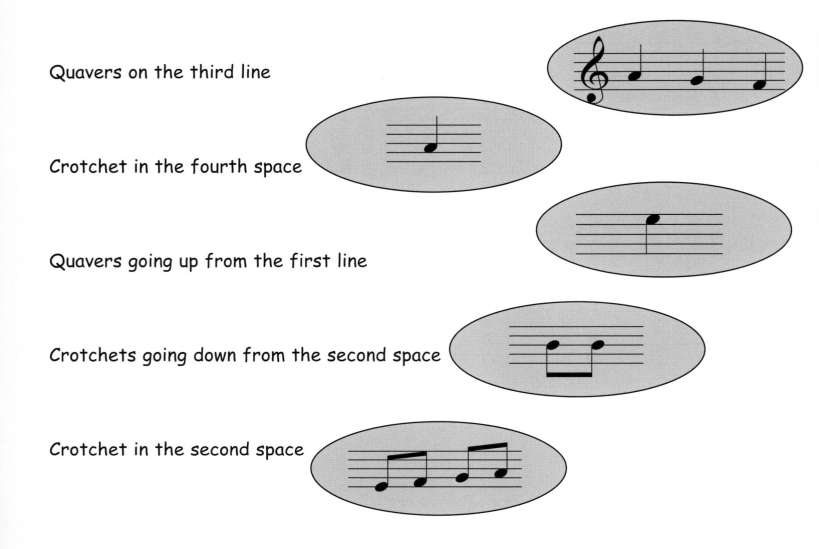

Quavers on the third line

Crotchet in the fourth space

Quavers going up from the first line

Crotchets going down from the second space

Crotchet in the second space

And now... can you draw the correct notes in the ovals?

Crotchets in the third space
(with stems going down like the letter 'p')

Quavers on the first line (with stems going up like the letter 'd')

Mystery Motifs

A 'motif' is a short melody or theme.

You'll hear these six motifs played in a certain order. Sing each one back after you hear it, and place a number from 1 to 6 in the boxes provided, in the order you hear them. Don't forget to listen for rests (silence) just as much as you listen for notes!

a.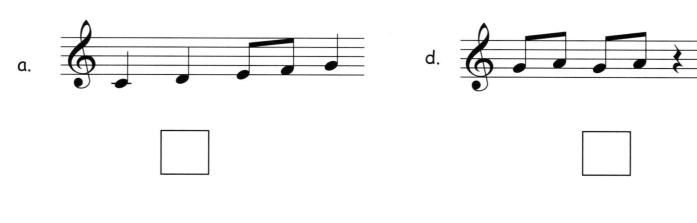

d.

b.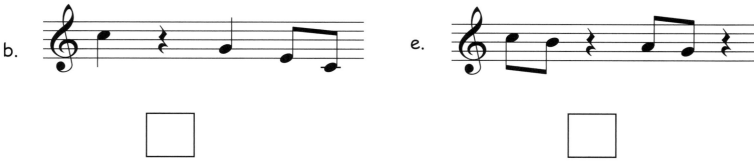

e.

c.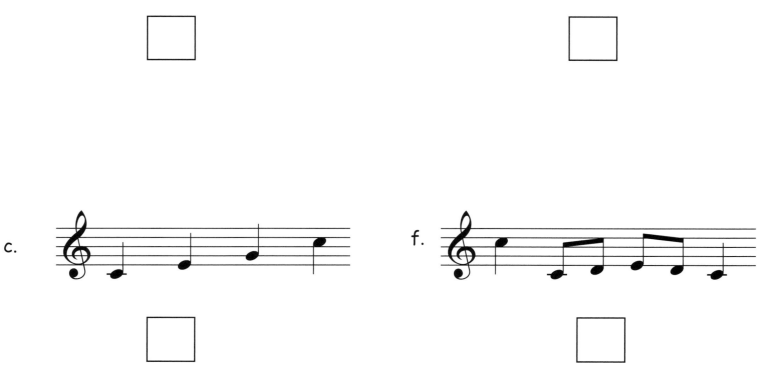

f.

Introducing F, G and A

F, G and A are three easy notes for our voices to sing.

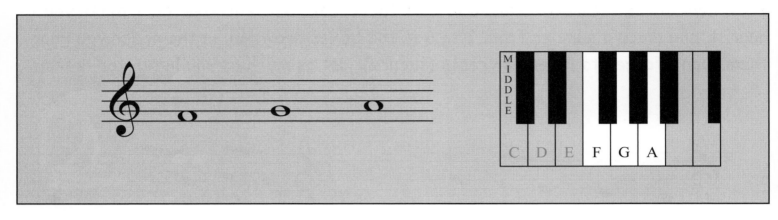

★ Have a go at singing the notes F, G and A as crotchets and quavers:

Crotchets   Quavers

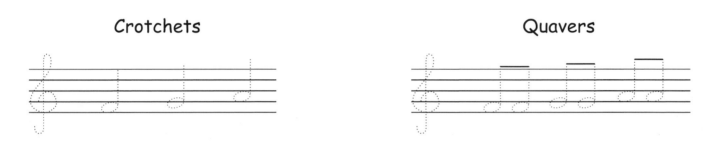

Now trace the treble clefs, notes and stems. (Don't forget to fill in the note heads!)

★ Can you name these notes correctly? Try listening and singing them back!

F   _   _   _   _   _   _   _   _   _   _   _

★ Write the letter names under these notes. Then listen and sing this melody too!

_   _   _   _   _   _   _   _   _   _

Singing with Numbers

When we sing note patterns starting on F, we can also sing 'F' as the number 1. So, F–G–A can also be sung as 1–2–3. Sing this:

F   G   A   1   2   3   A   G   F   3   2   1

Great work! When we sing in numbers it's called using 'scale-degree' numbers.

Here are some short melodies. For each, clap it first, then sing it using scale-degree numbers. After that, sing them again using letter names!

1.

5.

2.

6.

3.

7.

4.

8.

Notes and Numbers

Listen to and sing all of the motifs below, then match each one to the correct scale degrees. Watch out, things may match up across the two pages!

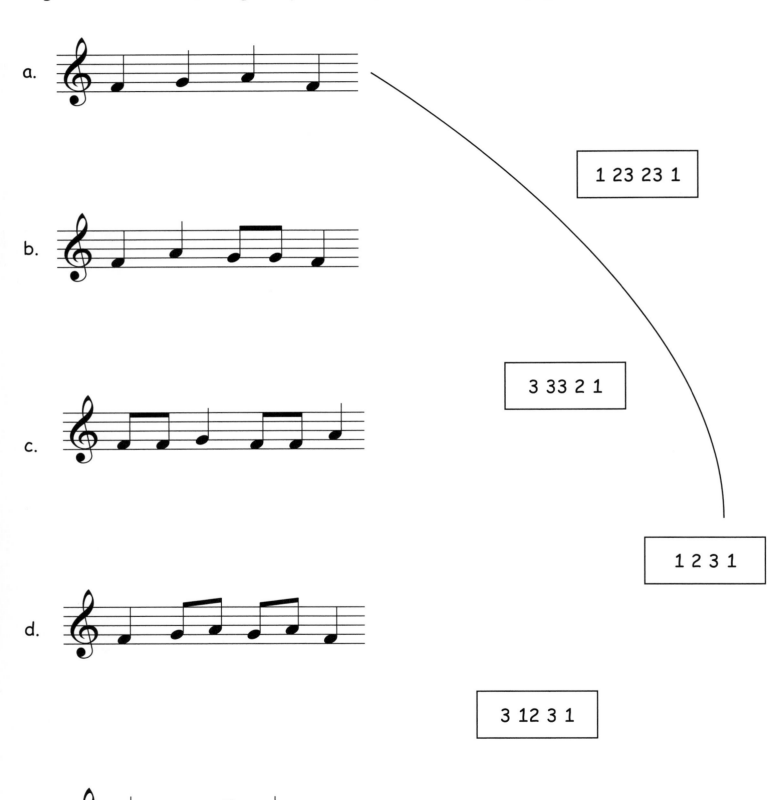

1 23 23 1

3 33 2 1

1 2 3 1

3 12 3 1

33 2 12 1

1 2 2 3

f.

33 1 23 1

g.

1 3 22 1

h.

31 23 31 2

i.

11 2 11 3

j.

 Final task: Sing some of these to a relative or friend and see if they can guess which one you're singing!!

G, A and B

Now we're going to sing some patterns that are a little higher. We'll start on G and go up to a new note: B.

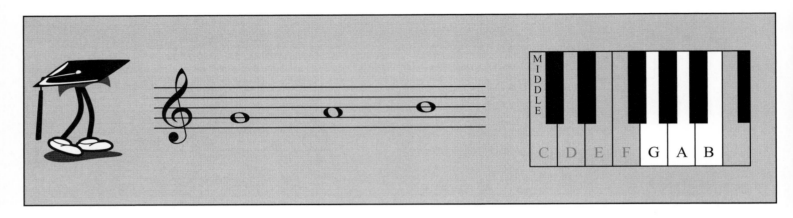

The pattern G–A–B can also be sung as 1-2-3. Sing this!

Now go back to page 13 and sing the first F-G-A pattern again. What do you notice?

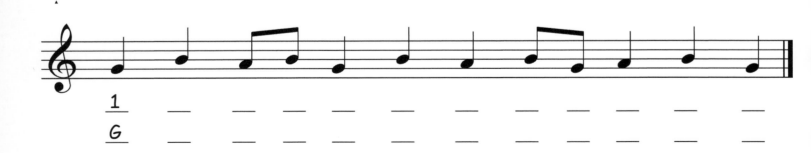

Can you sing the scale-degree numbers?

Can you write the correct letter names and scale-degree numbers under these notes?

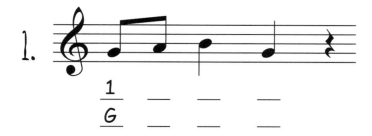

1.

$\frac{1}{G}$ — — —

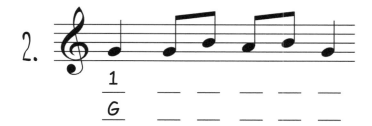

2.

$\frac{1}{G}$ — — — — —

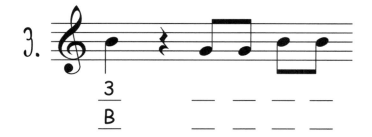

3.

$\frac{3}{B}$ — — — —

4.

$\frac{1}{G}$ — — — — —

5.

$\frac{3}{B}$ — — — —

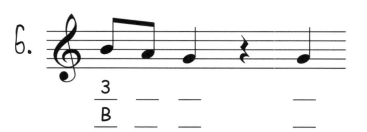

6.

$\frac{3}{B}$ — — —

Now sing all of the notes on this page!

Semiquavers

 = SEMIQUAVERS = one beat, four sounds

Semiquavers are twice as fast as quavers!

Count to four before you clap each one of these rhythms. But don't count in too fast, or the semiquavers will be too hard to clap!

1.

3.

2.

4.

Here are two melodies (each with a time signature and barlines – more about this later!) using F, G and A. Clap them and sing them!

1.

2.

Minims

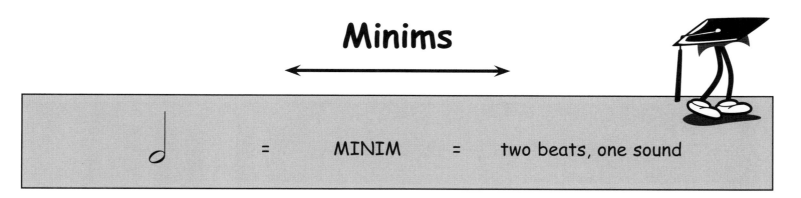

| | = | MINIM | = | two beats, one sound |

Minims are twice as long as crotchets.

Count to four before you clap each one of these rhythms.

Well done! Now here are some melodies to sing, all using G, A and B.

Middle C, D, and E

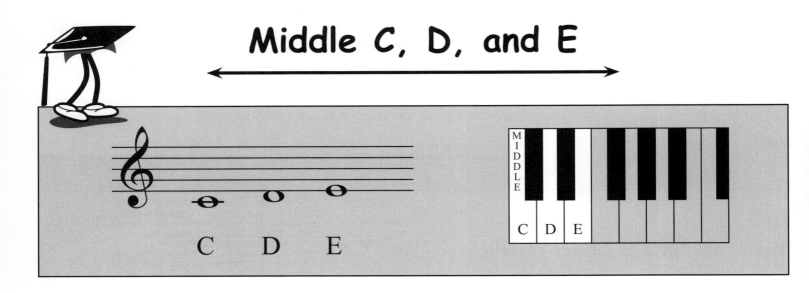

C   D   E

★ Here is a melody using the notes C, D and E. Clap it and sing it, then fill in the scale-degree numbers and letter names!

1
C

And now here are two more melodies... do it all again for both of them!

Great work! Now your teacher will play or sing these short melodies. Can you fill in the missing notes?

20

The C Major Scale

The C major scale consists of all the letter names from middle C up to the next C. It's super easy to sing! (Pssst: sing it now using letter names)

Look, here's our new note: high C!

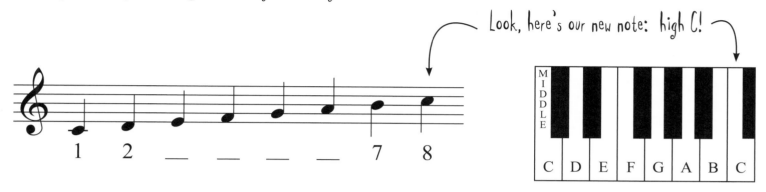

This scale is going down. It starts up high so take a big breath!

You've probably noticed that '8' has the same letter name as '1'. Most of the time you'll only use '1' when sight singing. Discuss this more with your teacher!

Here are some really easy melodies to sing, all based on the C major scale:

1.

2.

3.

Stems

★ Stems can go either up or down.

★ When stems go up, they always go on the right, like the letter 'd':

★ When stems go down, they always go on the left, like the letter 'p':

REMEMBER: 'd' for dogs and 'p' for puppies!

Apart from drawing stems on the correct side of the note, we also have to know when a stem goes up and when it goes down. There are three rules to remember:

Notes **BELOW** the middle line (third line) have their stems going **UP**.

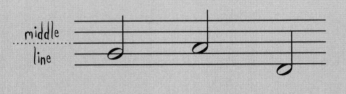

The stems go on the right, like the letter 'd'.

Notes **ABOVE** the middle line have their stems going **DOWN**.

The stems go on the left, like the letter 'p'.

Notes sitting **ON** the middle line can go up **OR** down – you can choose!

Remember 'd' for dogs and 'p' for puppies!

★ Are these stems on the correct side of the notes? Put a tick for 'yes' or a cross for 'no' on each. Remember, we want 'dogs' and 'puppies', not 'bogs' or 'quppies'!!!

★ Some of these stems are going up when they should be going down. Can you find the mistakes and put a big cross on them? (Remember: notes on the middle line can go up or down)

★ And now some of these stems are going down when they should be going up! Can you find the mistakes? (Remember: notes on the middle line can go up or down)

★ See if you can add stems correctly to these note heads. The stem must be going in the right direction AND must be on the correct side of the note!

Tunes with Words

These tunes are a little different from everything else you've sung so far... they have WORDS!

Before you sing each one, read the words, look at the shape of the melody and try to hear the sound of the notes in your head. All of them are in C major.

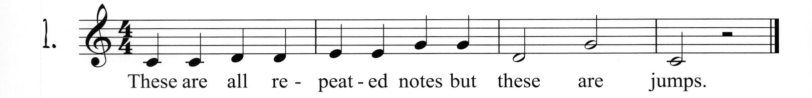

1. These are all re - peat - ed notes but these are jumps.

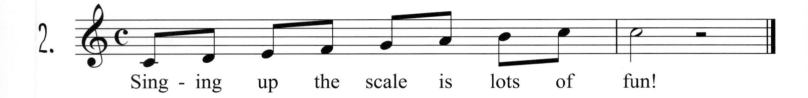

2. Sing - ing up the scale is lots of fun!

3. Com - ing down a - gain is just as good.

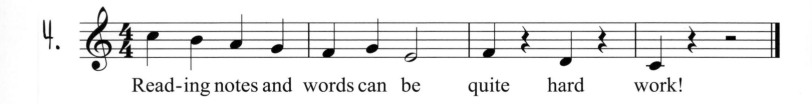

4. Read-ing notes and words can be quite hard work!

5. Long notes need great big breaths.

For Your Ears Only

1. Fill in the missing notes in the spots marked *, according to what you hear your teacher play.

a.

c.

b.

d.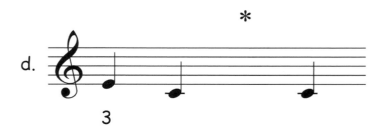

2. Now sing the melodies above!

3. Your teacher will now play four different sets of notes. Which scale-degree numbers do you hear?

1 __ __ __ 1   5 __ __ 5 __

3 __ __ __   3 2 __ __ __

4. Have a go at singing the melodies below. Then your teacher will play each one with some deliberate changes. Can you circle the notes that don't match???

25

Two New Rhythms

Here are two longer note values: the dotted minim and the semibreve.

𝅗𝅥. = DOTTED MINIM = three beats, one sound

𝅝 = SEMIBREVE = four beats, one sound

Clap these rhythms. Count to four before you clap each of them.

And now for some musical maths! Add up the number of beats in each question.

1. 𝅗𝅥 + 𝅗𝅥. = ___

2. ♩ + ♬♬ = ___

3. ♫ + 𝄽 + 𝅗𝅥 = ___

4. ♫ + 𝅝 = ___

5. 𝄽 + ♩ + ♫ = ___

6. 𝅝 + 𝄽 = ___

7. ♫ + 𝅗𝅥. = ___

8. ♬♬ + ♫ = ___

Be Creative

Invent your own eight-beat rhythm here. The line in the middle is a 'barline' (more about this later). Create your rhythm so that you have four beats in each 'bar' – that is, four beats on either side of the bar line!

Have you clapped it? Good work! Now, the rhythms below are interesting... they are designed to be clapped together, as two parts! Try them:

1. With a friend and swap parts

2. On your own: top part on your right knee, bottom part on your left knee (tricky, eh?)

And for your final creative challenge... here is a melody with one beat missing in each bar. At the places marked * choose C, E, or G (you may use one crotchet or two quavers) to fill the missing beats. Then try to sing it and see if you like it!

Beat Bingo

You'll need a single die to play this game.

Object of Game: To see if you can get 'Bingo' by crossing off all your beats with no more than ten rolls of the die. Here's how to play:

1. Roll the die to see how many 'beats' you should cross off.

2. Cross off the correct number of beats. For example, if you roll a 3, cross off three beats. You can choose whether you cross off three crotchets or a crotchet and a minim.

3. After each roll of the die, fill in one of the circles.

4. See if you can cross off all the beats before all the circles get filled in!

Rules: Every time you roll the die you MUST fill in a circle, even if you can't cross anything off. For example, if you roll a '1' and you have no crotchets left, you won't be able to cross anything off... but it still counts as a turn, and you must fill in a circle.

You may cross off fewer beats than you roll, but not more beats. For instance, if you roll a '3' and you only have minims and semibreves left, you may cross off just the minim and nothing else. Don't forget to fill in a circle!

When you've finished these games, go to **www.blitzbooks.com** and download some more!!!

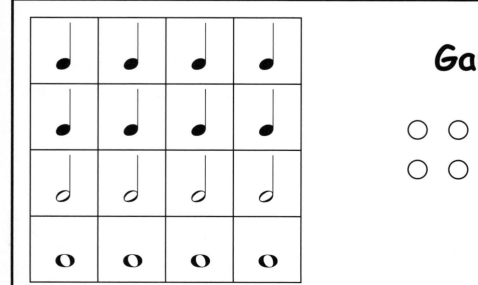

Game 1

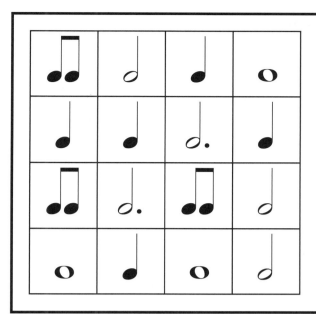

Game 2

○ ○ ○ ○ ○
○ ○ ○ ○ ○

Game 3

○ ○ ○ ○ ○
○ ○ ○ ○ ○

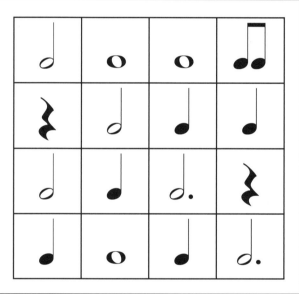

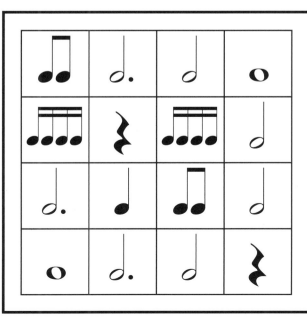

Game 4

○ ○ ○ ○ ○
○ ○ ○ ○ ○

More Mystery Motifs

Just like you did a while ago on page 11, you'll be numbering these motifs from 1 to 10 in the order you hear them. Watch out: some of the motifs have the same rhythms but different pitches, or the same pitch but different rhythms!

Two New Rests

⟷

▬	=	MINIM REST	=	two beats of silence
▬	=	SEMIBREVE REST or WHOLE-BAR REST	=	whole bar of silence

Minim rests and whole-bar rests have special positions on a staff.

A minim rest sits on the third line, like this:

A semibreve rest or whole bar rest hangs from the fourth line, like this:

The semibreve rest or whole-bar rest (▬) represents a whole bar of silence, no matter how many beats. It is like a joker in a pack of cards: it changes its value according to the 'time signature' (see page 36). When you play 'Beat Bingo II' on page 39, you'll notice that this rest has a different value in each game!

★ Can you fill in the missing information in this table?

REST	NAME OR NAMES	NUMBER OF BEATS	DESCRIPTION
𝄽			Like a 'Z' and a 'C' joined together
▬			A block that sits on the third line
▬		whole bar	A block that hangs from the fourth line

Let's Draw Rests

Crotchet Rests

Think of the crotchet rest as starting off a bit like the letter 'Z' with the letter 'C' springing off the bottom. It must start in the top space and finish in the bottom space. Trace and draw some crotchet rests on this staff:

Minim Rests

Minim rests sit on the **third** line of the staff. They must not take up the whole space between the lines. Draw them like this not like this!

Trace, draw and fill in some minim rests:

Whole-Bar Rests (Semibreve Rests)

Whole-bar rests hang from the **fourth** line and like minim rests must not take up the whole space! Trace, draw and fill in some whole bar rests here:

More Stuff to Sing

You'll get a starting note or chord from your teacher for each one of these melodies.

They don't all start on the same note, but they DO all start on scale-degree 1. This is to give you practice singing in different 'keys' (more about this later).

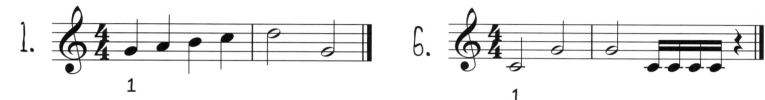

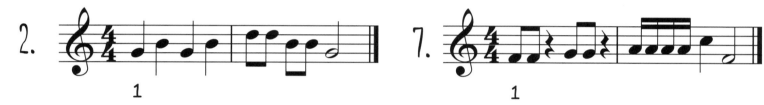

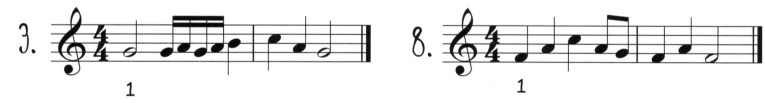

Melody Wheel

Starting at number 1, clap the rhythms all the way around the wheel without stopping. Then do it again, this time singing the melodies (which are all in 'F major', which is why there is a symbol after the clef – discuss this with your teacher!).

Then... work your way around the wheel again, either singing or clapping (or both), starting at any number you like!

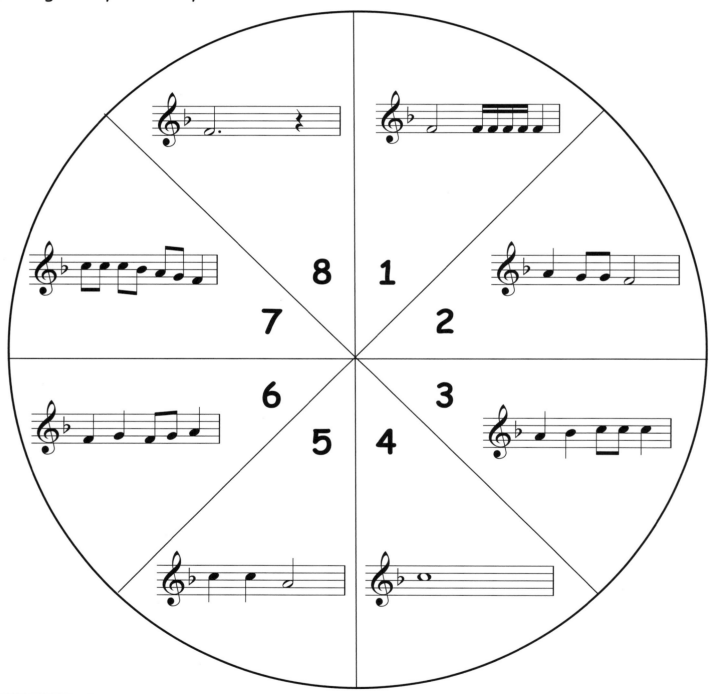

You can use this melody wheel in SOOOO many ways – to sing long tunes, to sing with friends, to compose your own pieces... the list is endless. Go to **www.blitzbooks.com** for some more great ideas!

Revision of Stuff

1. How many crotchets are there in a minim? _____

2. Name these notes:

_____   _____   _____

3. Draw a treble clef. Then draw these notes, each with the correct rhythm value.

E	high C	D	G	F
2 beats	4 beats	1 beat	2 beats	1 beat

4. How many minims are there in a semibreve? _____

5. Draw a minim rest in the correct position on this staff: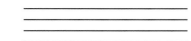

6. Name these treble-clef notes. Then re-write them with the stems going in the right direction! (Hint: not all of them are wrong!)

_____ _____ _____ _____ _____

Time Signatures and Barlines

Time signatures and barlines are an extremely important part of music. Without them, it would be hard to play any sort of rhythm.

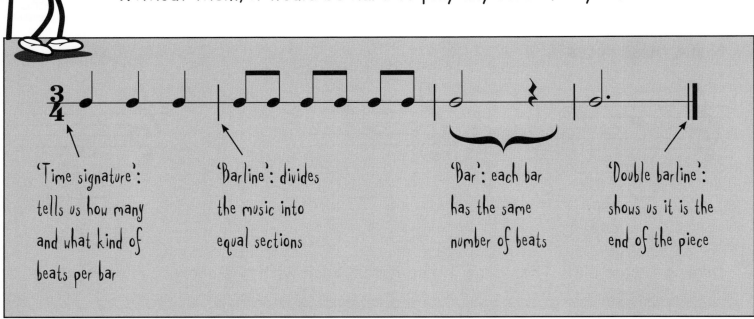

'Time signature': tells us how many and what kind of beats per bar

'Barline': divides the music into equal sections

'Bar': each bar has the same number of beats

'Double barline': shows us it is the end of the piece

Time Signatures

A time signature gives us information about the rhythm of a piece. The top number tells us the **number** of beats, and the bottom number tells us what **kind** of beat.

The time signatures ²⁄₄, ³⁄₄, and ⁴⁄₄ all have a '4' on the bottom, meaning 'crotchet' beats.

²⁄₄ means 'two crotchet beats per bar'. Here's a rhythm for you to clap:

★ Count up the number of beats in each bar. Does each bar have the same number of beats?

$\frac{3}{4}$ means 'three crotchet beats per bar'. Try clapping this rhythm:

★ Count the beats in each bar. Does every bar add up to three beats?

$\frac{4}{4}$ means 'four crotchet beats per bar'. Now clap this rhythm:

★ Check the number of beats in each bar. Do you find four beats in each?

Another very common time signature is this: **C**. That's right, it's the letter 'C', and this time signature is called 'common time'. **C** is exactly the same as $\frac{4}{4}$.

So **C** = common time = $\frac{4}{4}$ = four crotchet beats per bar! (phew!)

Here's another rhythm to clap, in common time:

★ Once again, count up the beats in each bar. There should be four!

And now for a challenge... can you figure out the time signature of these rhythms? Clap them for your teacher, then write the time signatures at the beginning!

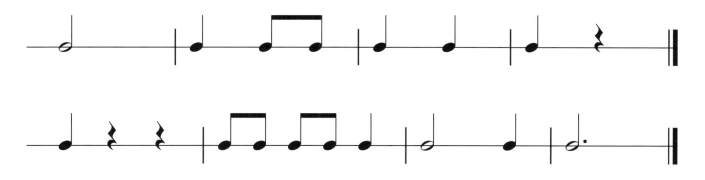

Be More Creative

Write your own four-bar rhythm here, putting three beats in each bar. Try to use a good mixture of all the rhythms and rests you've learned so far!

$\frac{3}{4}$ | | | ‖

If you use the rhythm you just composed, and decide on a note for each rhythm value, you can actually compose your own melody! (How cool is THAT!)

Try this on the staff below. If you stick to the letter names below each bar (you can use them in any order) it will help to make your melody sound really good. So, for bar 1, only use the notes C, E and G, and for bar 2 choose only from F, A and C, and so on!

BIG TIP: Make sure your melody ends on a C – this will sound great.

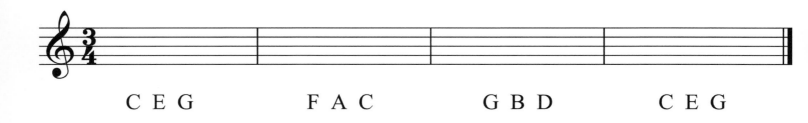

C E G   F A C   G B D   C E G

COMPOSITION CHALLENGE: Make up four short melodies using the time signatures $\frac{2}{4}$, $\frac{3}{4}$, $\frac{4}{4}$ and C! You can download free manuscript paper from www.blitzbooks.com

Beat Bingo II (see rules on p.28)

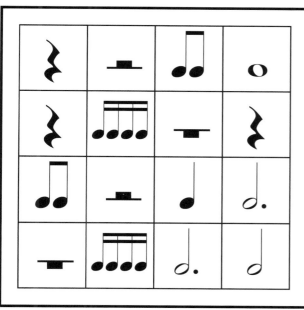

Game 1

○ ○ ○ ○ ○
○ ○ ○ ○ ○

(In this game, 𝄽 = 4)

Game 2

○ ○ ○ ○ ○
○ ○ ○ ○ ○

(In this game, 𝄽 = 3)

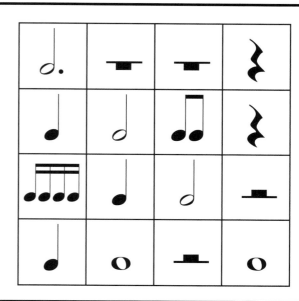

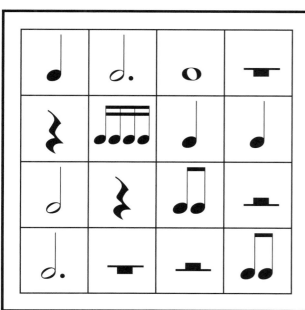

Game 3

○ ○ ○ ○ ○
○ ○ ○ ○ ○

(In this game, 𝄽 = 4)

Create a Canon

A 'canon' is like a round. It's a melody that can be sung by two or more people, starting at different times. Your teacher has probably sung a few canons or rounds with you (perhaps even with the 'melody wheel' back on page 34!).

Here is a canon. Sing it through using scale-degree numbers. When you try it with your friends, a new person starts from the beginning every three beats!

Guess what? You are going to make up your own canon (yes, that's right!). Just choose from the notes C, E and G (and high C) for each of the rhythm values given. You can't go wrong – sing it with your friends and it will sound terrific!

Be the Teacher

Lucky for you, someone has already filled in the answers on this page. BUT... some of them are wrong! Your job is to be the teacher and mark these questions. Have fun!

1. Write the correct beat value under each of these (1 mark each):

2. Write the correct notes for these letter names (1 mark each):

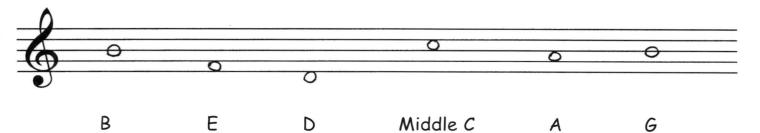

B   E   D   Middle C   A   G

3. Add stems to these notes (2 marks each):

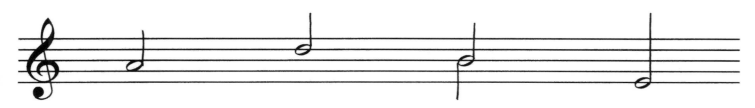

Total:

Now go to **www.blitzbooks.com** and download the 'Be the Teacher_Sight Singing' page. Do the page without peeking at this one and see if you can get full marks!

C, F and G major

You may not realise it, but you have become very good at singing melodies in three different keys – C major, F major and G major – where either C, F, or G is number 1.

Well, each of these keys has it's own special signature, to let you know which note is number 1. This is a called a **key signature,** and it is always written after the clef.

This is the key signature of C major:  There is just a treble clef here! C major has the simplest key signature... nothing!

This is the key signature of F major:  This is called a 'B flat'. All pieces in F major have this symbol after the clef

This is the key signature of G major:  This is called an 'F sharp'. All pieces in G major have this symbol after the clef

Can you name the key of these melodies? Once you've done that, you'll know which note is number 1, and you can sing them!

Very important tip: Melodies can begin on any scale-degree number, but they nearly always END on number 1!

Let's Sing in Keys!

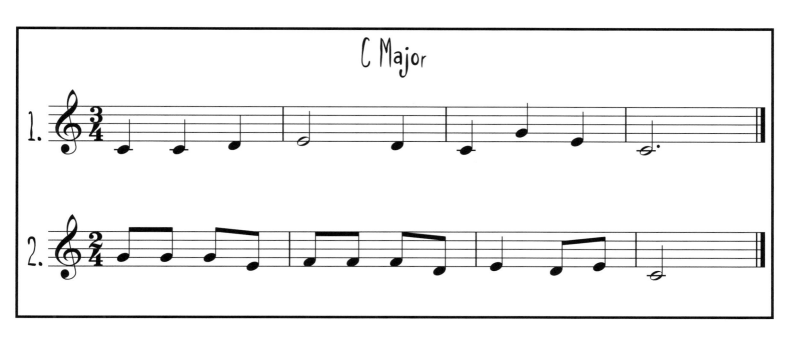

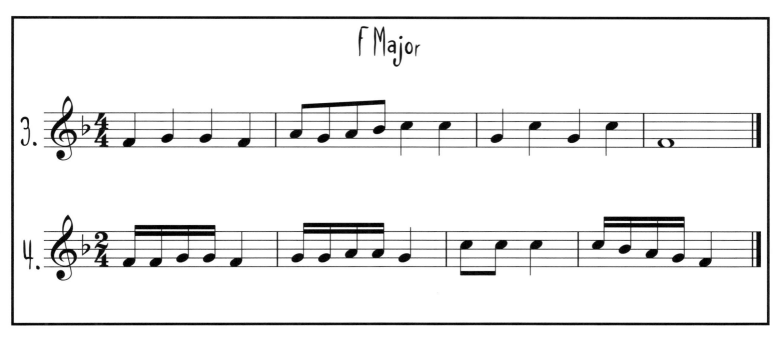

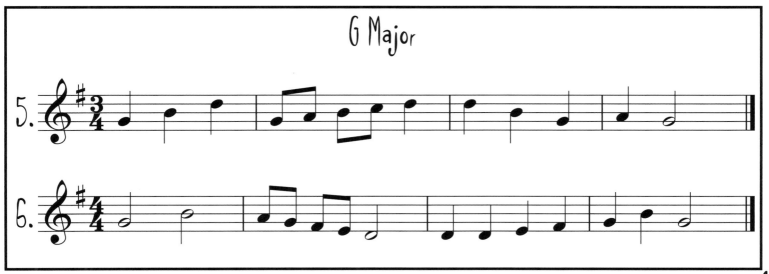

Groovy Games

1. Note Tally

For this game you will need a stopwatch or timer.

Here are three notes – they happen to be scale-degrees 1, 3 and 5 of F major.

Your teacher will play or sing each note a few times so you can get used to the sound of them. Then, once your teacher says 'go', you'll need to keep a tally (by putting a stroke or dot in the box) of how many times you hear each note in one minute!

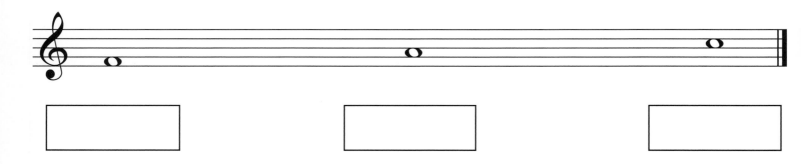

2. Find-a-Word

For this game you'll need your best note-reading skills.

See if you can find the words listed below. But this is no ordinary find-a-word... the words are written as music notes! (oooooaahh!)

G	D	F	C	A	B	G	E
D	F	A	B	B	G	D	A
E	D	D	A	B	B	E	D
G	E	E	D	C	A	G	E
A	C	D	D	A	B	G	E
B	A	G	G	A	G	E	D
B	F	E	F	E	E	B	B
A	B	G	G	B	A	B	E
C	E	G	B	A	D	G	E

44

Two-Part Tunes

Sight Singing Whiz Waltz

Two-Part Tango

Remarkable Rounds

This round is usually sung with words... but it's a great idea to sing it with scale-degree numbers instead! It is one of the rare tunes that does not end on no. 1. Each person can start after eight bars, or even every four bars!

This round works in lots of different ways, with lots of people! Each person can start after one bar, or half a bar, or even just one crotchet beat! Another fun thing to do is to replace one of the numbers with a clap.

*8 can be sung as 1 instead

Cool Canons

All of the canons below can be performed with a new part entering every bar.

Lyn Williams

1 2 3 4 5   This is high 5   1 7 6 5   This is low 5

High 5 low 5   High D low D   5 4 3 2 1   5 6 7 1

Thomas Tallis

Lyn Williams

Now the sun has gone a___ way   And we greet the end of the day___

Moon is ri - sing stars are shi - ning Trees bend and gen___ tly sway

Congratulations!

You have just completed

'How To Blitz! Sight Singing!'

Name: _____

Teacher's signature: _____

Parent's signature: _____

How To ~~Pass~~ BLITZ!

www.blitzbooks.com